THIS BOOK
BELONGS TO

Classroom Expense Log

MONTH   **YEAR**

CLASS

DATE	ITEM	DESCRIPTION	CATEGORY	AMOUNT

Classroom Expense Log

MONTH

YEAR

CLASS

DATE	ITEM	DESCRIPTION	CATEGORY	AMOUNT

Classroom Expense Log

MONTH   **YEAR**

CLASS

DATE	ITEM	DESCRIPTION	CATEGORY	AMOUNT

Classroom Expense Log

MONTH　　　　　　　　　　**YEAR**

CLASS

DATE	ITEM	DESCRIPTION	CATEGORY	AMOUNT

Classroom Expense Log

MONTH   **YEAR**

CLASS

DATE	ITEM	DESCRIPTION	CATEGORY	AMOUNT

Classroom Expense Log

MONTH **YEAR**

CLASS

DATE	ITEM	DESCRIPTION	CATEGORY	AMOUNT

Classroom Expense Log

MONTH   **YEAR**

CLASS

DATE	ITEM	DESCRIPTION	CATEGORY	AMOUNT

Classroom Expense Log

MONTH

YEAR

CLASS

DATE	ITEM	DESCRIPTION	CATEGORY	AMOUNT

Classroom Expense Log

MONTH   **YEAR**

CLASS

DATE	ITEM	DESCRIPTION	CATEGORY	AMOUNT

Classroom Expense Log

MONTH   **YEAR**

CLASS

DATE	ITEM	DESCRIPTION	CATEGORY	AMOUNT

Classroom Expense Log

MONTH   **YEAR**

CLASS

DATE	ITEM	DESCRIPTION	CATEGORY	AMOUNT

Classroom Expense Log

MONTH **YEAR**

CLASS

DATE	ITEM	DESCRIPTION	CATEGORY	AMOUNT

Classroom Expense Log

MONTH

YEAR

CLASS

DATE	ITEM	DESCRIPTION	CATEGORY	AMOUNT

Classroom Expense Log

MONTH **YEAR**

CLASS

DATE	ITEM	DESCRIPTION	CATEGORY	AMOUNT

Classroom Expense Log

MONTH   **YEAR**

CLASS

DATE	ITEM	DESCRIPTION	CATEGORY	AMOUNT

Classroom Expense Log

MONTH   **YEAR**

CLASS

DATE	ITEM	DESCRIPTION	CATEGORY	AMOUNT

Classroom Expense Log

MONTH   **YEAR**

CLASS

DATE	ITEM	DESCRIPTION	CATEGORY	AMOUNT

Classroom Expense Log

MONTH   YEAR

CLASS

DATE	ITEM	DESCRIPTION	CATEGORY	AMOUNT

Classroom Expense Log

MONTH   **YEAR**

CLASS

DATE	ITEM	DESCRIPTION	CATEGORY	AMOUNT

Classroom Expense Log

MONTH　　　　　　　　　　**YEAR**

CLASS

DATE	ITEM	DESCRIPTION	CATEGORY	AMOUNT

Classroom Expense Log

MONTH   **YEAR**

CLASS

DATE	ITEM	DESCRIPTION	CATEGORY	AMOUNT

Classroom Expense Log

MONTH   **YEAR**

CLASS

DATE	ITEM	DESCRIPTION	CATEGORY	AMOUNT

Classroom Expense Log

MONTH   **YEAR**

CLASS

DATE	ITEM	DESCRIPTION	CATEGORY	AMOUNT

Classroom Expense Log

MONTH   **YEAR**

CLASS

DATE	ITEM	DESCRIPTION	CATEGORY	AMOUNT

Classroom Expense Log

DATE	ITEM	DESCRIPTION	CATEGORY	AMOUNT

Classroom Expense Log

MONTH   **YEAR**

CLASS

DATE	ITEM	DESCRIPTION	CATEGORY	AMOUNT

Classroom Expense Log

MONTH   **YEAR**

CLASS

DATE	ITEM	DESCRIPTION	CATEGORY	AMOUNT

Classroom Expense Log

MONTH   **YEAR**

CLASS

DATE	ITEM	DESCRIPTION	CATEGORY	AMOUNT

Classroom Expense Log

MONTH   **YEAR**

CLASS

DATE	ITEM	DESCRIPTION	CATEGORY	AMOUNT

Classroom Expense Log

MONTH   **YEAR**

CLASS

DATE	ITEM	DESCRIPTION	CATEGORY	AMOUNT

Classroom Expense Log

MONTH   **YEAR**

CLASS

DATE	ITEM	DESCRIPTION	CATEGORY	AMOUNT

Classroom Expense Log

MONTH **YEAR**

CLASS

DATE	ITEM	DESCRIPTION	CATEGORY	AMOUNT

Classroom Expense Log

MONTH   **YEAR**

CLASS

DATE	ITEM	DESCRIPTION	CATEGORY	AMOUNT

Classroom Expense Log

MONTH   **YEAR**

CLASS

DATE	ITEM	DESCRIPTION	CATEGORY	AMOUNT

Classroom Expense Log

MONTH   YEAR

CLASS

DATE	ITEM	DESCRIPTION	CATEGORY	AMOUNT

Classroom Expense Log

MONTH

YEAR

CLASS

DATE	ITEM	DESCRIPTION	CATEGORY	AMOUNT

Classroom Expense Log

MONTH   **YEAR**

CLASS

DATE	ITEM	DESCRIPTION	CATEGORY	AMOUNT

Classroom Expense Log

MONTH   **YEAR**

CLASS

DATE	ITEM	DESCRIPTION	CATEGORY	AMOUNT

Classroom Expense Log

MONTH　　　　　　　　　　**YEAR**

CLASS

DATE	ITEM	DESCRIPTION	CATEGORY	AMOUNT

Classroom Expense Log

MONTH **YEAR**

CLASS

DATE	ITEM	DESCRIPTION	CATEGORY	AMOUNT

Classroom Expense Log

MONTH   **YEAR**

CLASS

DATE	ITEM	DESCRIPTION	CATEGORY	AMOUNT

Classroom Expense Log

MONTH   **YEAR**

CLASS

DATE	ITEM	DESCRIPTION	CATEGORY	AMOUNT

Classroom Expense Log

MONTH ____________________ YEAR ____________________

CLASS ____________________

DATE	ITEM	DESCRIPTION	CATEGORY	AMOUNT

Classroom Expense Log

MONTH   **YEAR**

CLASS

DATE	ITEM	DESCRIPTION	CATEGORY	AMOUNT

Classroom Expense Log

MONTH   **YEAR**

CLASS

DATE	ITEM	DESCRIPTION	CATEGORY	AMOUNT

Classroom Expense Log

MONTH　　　　　　　　　　**YEAR**

CLASS

DATE	ITEM	DESCRIPTION	CATEGORY	AMOUNT

Classroom Expense Log

MONTH   **YEAR**

CLASS

DATE	ITEM	DESCRIPTION	CATEGORY	AMOUNT

Classroom Expense Log

MONTH   **YEAR**

CLASS

DATE	ITEM	DESCRIPTION	CATEGORY	AMOUNT

Classroom Expense Log

MONTH　　　　　　　　　　**YEAR**

CLASS

DATE	ITEM	DESCRIPTION	CATEGORY	AMOUNT

Classroom Expense Log

MONTH   **YEAR**

CLASS

DATE	ITEM	DESCRIPTION	CATEGORY	AMOUNT

Classroom Expense Log

MONTH   **YEAR**

CLASS

DATE	ITEM	DESCRIPTION	CATEGORY	AMOUNT

Classroom Expense Log

MONTH

YEAR

CLASS

DATE	ITEM	DESCRIPTION	CATEGORY	AMOUNT

Classroom Expense Log

MONTH **YEAR**

CLASS

DATE	ITEM	DESCRIPTION	CATEGORY	AMOUNT

Classroom Expense Log

MONTH **YEAR**

CLASS

DATE	ITEM	DESCRIPTION	CATEGORY	AMOUNT

Classroom Expense Log

MONTH   **YEAR**

CLASS

DATE	ITEM	DESCRIPTION	CATEGORY	AMOUNT

Classroom Expense Log

MONTH   **YEAR**

CLASS

DATE	ITEM	DESCRIPTION	CATEGORY	AMOUNT

Classroom Expense Log

MONTH ____________________ YEAR ____________________

CLASS ____________________

DATE	ITEM	DESCRIPTION	CATEGORY	AMOUNT

Classroom Expense Log

MONTH   **YEAR**

CLASS

DATE	ITEM	DESCRIPTION	CATEGORY	AMOUNT

Classroom Expense Log

MONTH   YEAR

CLASS

DATE	ITEM	DESCRIPTION	CATEGORY	AMOUNT

Classroom Expense Log

MONTH

YEAR

CLASS

DATE	ITEM	DESCRIPTION	CATEGORY	AMOUNT

Classroom Expense Log

MONTH   **YEAR**

CLASS

DATE	ITEM	DESCRIPTION	CATEGORY	AMOUNT

Classroom Expense Log

MONTH   **YEAR**

CLASS

DATE	ITEM	DESCRIPTION	CATEGORY	AMOUNT

Classroom Expense Log

MONTH   **YEAR**

CLASS

DATE	ITEM	DESCRIPTION	CATEGORY	AMOUNT

Classroom Expense Log

MONTH   **YEAR**

CLASS

DATE	ITEM	DESCRIPTION	CATEGORY	AMOUNT

Classroom Expense Log

MONTH   YEAR

CLASS

DATE	ITEM	DESCRIPTION	CATEGORY	AMOUNT

Classroom Expense Log

MONTH　　　　　　　　　**YEAR**

CLASS

DATE	ITEM	DESCRIPTION	CATEGORY	AMOUNT

Classroom Expense Log

MONTH **YEAR**

CLASS

DATE	ITEM	DESCRIPTION	CATEGORY	AMOUNT

Classroom Expense Log

MONTH   **YEAR**

CLASS

DATE	ITEM	DESCRIPTION	CATEGORY	AMOUNT

Classroom Expense Log

MONTH   YEAR

CLASS

DATE	ITEM	DESCRIPTION	CATEGORY	AMOUNT

Classroom Expense Log

MONTH   **YEAR**

CLASS

DATE	ITEM	DESCRIPTION	CATEGORY	AMOUNT

Classroom Expense Log

MONTH   **YEAR**

CLASS

DATE	ITEM	DESCRIPTION	CATEGORY	AMOUNT

Classroom Expense Log

MONTH   YEAR

CLASS

DATE	ITEM	DESCRIPTION	CATEGORY	AMOUNT

Classroom Expense Log

MONTH

YEAR

CLASS

DATE	ITEM	DESCRIPTION	CATEGORY	AMOUNT

Classroom Expense Log

MONTH   **YEAR**

CLASS

DATE	ITEM	DESCRIPTION	CATEGORY	AMOUNT

Classroom Expense Log

MONTH

YEAR

CLASS

DATE	ITEM	DESCRIPTION	CATEGORY	AMOUNT

Classroom Expense Log

MONTH   **YEAR**

CLASS

DATE	ITEM	DESCRIPTION	CATEGORY	AMOUNT

Classroom Expense Log

MONTH ___________________   **YEAR** ___________________

CLASS ___________________

DATE	ITEM	DESCRIPTION	CATEGORY	AMOUNT

Classroom Expense Log

MONTH

YEAR

CLASS

DATE	ITEM	DESCRIPTION	CATEGORY	AMOUNT

Classroom Expense Log

MONTH   **YEAR**

CLASS

DATE	ITEM	DESCRIPTION	CATEGORY	AMOUNT

Classroom Expense Log

MONTH   **YEAR**

CLASS

DATE	ITEM	DESCRIPTION	CATEGORY	AMOUNT

Classroom Expense Log

MONTH   **YEAR**

CLASS

DATE	ITEM	DESCRIPTION	CATEGORY	AMOUNT

Classroom Expense Log

MONTH **YEAR**

CLASS

DATE	ITEM	DESCRIPTION	CATEGORY	AMOUNT

Classroom Expense Log

MONTH   **YEAR**

CLASS

DATE	ITEM	DESCRIPTION	CATEGORY	AMOUNT

Classroom Expense Log

MONTH **YEAR**

CLASS

DATE	ITEM	DESCRIPTION	CATEGORY	AMOUNT

Classroom Expense Log

MONTH   **YEAR**

CLASS

DATE	ITEM	DESCRIPTION	CATEGORY	AMOUNT

Classroom Expense Log

MONTH　　　　　　　　**YEAR**

CLASS

DATE	ITEM	DESCRIPTION	CATEGORY	AMOUNT

Classroom Expense Log

MONTH   **YEAR**

CLASS

DATE	ITEM	DESCRIPTION	CATEGORY	AMOUNT

Classroom Expense Log

MONTH   **YEAR**

CLASS

DATE	ITEM	DESCRIPTION	CATEGORY	AMOUNT

Classroom Expense Log

MONTH   **YEAR**

CLASS

DATE	ITEM	DESCRIPTION	CATEGORY	AMOUNT

Classroom Expense Log

MONTH   **YEAR**

CLASS

DATE	ITEM	DESCRIPTION	CATEGORY	AMOUNT

Classroom Expense Log

MONTH ___________________________ YEAR ___________________

CLASS ____

DATE	ITEM	DESCRIPTION	CATEGORY	AMOUNT

Classroom Expense Log

MONTH   **YEAR**

CLASS

DATE	ITEM	DESCRIPTION	CATEGORY	AMOUNT

Classroom Expense Log

MONTH   **YEAR**

CLASS

DATE	ITEM	DESCRIPTION	CATEGORY	AMOUNT

Classroom Expense Log

MONTH   **YEAR**

CLASS

DATE	ITEM	DESCRIPTION	CATEGORY	AMOUNT

Classroom Expense Log

MONTH   **YEAR**

CLASS

DATE	ITEM	DESCRIPTION	CATEGORY	AMOUNT

Classroom Expense Log

MONTH   **YEAR**

CLASS

DATE	ITEM	DESCRIPTION	CATEGORY	AMOUNT

Classroom Expense Log

MONTH   **YEAR**

CLASS

DATE	ITEM	DESCRIPTION	CATEGORY	AMOUNT

Classroom Expense Log

MONTH   **YEAR**

CLASS

DATE	ITEM	DESCRIPTION	CATEGORY	AMOUNT

Classroom Expense Log

MONTH　　　　　　　　　　**YEAR**

CLASS

DATE	ITEM	DESCRIPTION	CATEGORY	AMOUNT

Classroom Expense Log

MONTH   **YEAR**

CLASS

DATE	ITEM	DESCRIPTION	CATEGORY	AMOUNT

Classroom Expense Log

MONTH   **YEAR**

CLASS

DATE	ITEM	DESCRIPTION	CATEGORY	AMOUNT

Classroom Expense Log

MONTH   **YEAR**

CLASS

DATE	ITEM	DESCRIPTION	CATEGORY	AMOUNT

Classroom Expense Log

MONTH   **YEAR**

CLASS

DATE	ITEM	DESCRIPTION	CATEGORY	AMOUNT

Classroom Expense Log

MONTH   YEAR

CLASS

DATE	ITEM	DESCRIPTION	CATEGORY	AMOUNT

Classroom Expense Log

MONTH   **YEAR**

CLASS

DATE	ITEM	DESCRIPTION	CATEGORY	AMOUNT

Classroom Expense Log

MONTH   **YEAR**

CLASS

DATE	ITEM	DESCRIPTION	CATEGORY	AMOUNT

Classroom Expense Log

MONTH   **YEAR**

CLASS

DATE	ITEM	DESCRIPTION	CATEGORY	AMOUNT

Classroom Expense Log

MONTH   **YEAR**

CLASS

DATE	ITEM	DESCRIPTION	CATEGORY	AMOUNT

Classroom Expense Log

MONTH **YEAR**

CLASS

DATE	ITEM	DESCRIPTION	CATEGORY	AMOUNT

Classroom Expense Log

MONTH   **YEAR**

CLASS

DATE	ITEM	DESCRIPTION	CATEGORY	AMOUNT

Classroom Expense Log

MONTH   **YEAR**

CLASS

DATE	ITEM	DESCRIPTION	CATEGORY	AMOUNT

Classroom Expense Log

MONTH   **YEAR**

CLASS

DATE	ITEM	DESCRIPTION	CATEGORY	AMOUNT

Classroom Expense Log

MONTH   **YEAR**

CLASS

DATE	ITEM	DESCRIPTION	CATEGORY	AMOUNT

Classroom Expense Log

MONTH
YEAR
CLASS

DATE	ITEM	DESCRIPTION	CATEGORY	AMOUNT

Classroom Expense Log

MONTH　　　　　　　　**YEAR**

CLASS

DATE	ITEM	DESCRIPTION	CATEGORY	AMOUNT

Classroom Expense Log

MONTH   **YEAR**

CLASS

DATE	ITEM	DESCRIPTION	CATEGORY	AMOUNT

Classroom Expense Log

MONTH   YEAR

CLASS

DATE	ITEM	DESCRIPTION	CATEGORY	AMOUNT

Classroom Expense Log

MONTH   **YEAR**

CLASS

DATE	ITEM	DESCRIPTION	CATEGORY	AMOUNT

Classroom Expense Log

MONTH   **YEAR**

CLASS

DATE	ITEM	DESCRIPTION	CATEGORY	AMOUNT